Poems :

Who Care

A collection of heartfelt and emotional poems about caring for loved ones including messages of hope and advice for those on the same journey

By

Patrick J McTaggart

Poems in Celebration of Carers Worldwide
For the love and compassion they show and their dedication in caring for those they love.

ISBN: 9798373817240

Contents

Introduction

In 2022 I published a collection of poems in the book "Our Dementia Journey" charting my family's experiences with dementia since my Dad's diagnosis.

My Dad, also called Pat, was diagnosed with dementia several years ago. Over the last couple of years my Mum's health has deteriorated from a physical perspective and she now has no mobility and suffers from a deal of pain. I live with my parents and am the main carer for them both, having retired early from my job in finance. The journey we are on since Dad was diagnosed with dementia is very much a family affair for Dad, my Mum Margaret, my sister Donna and my brother Steven.

As a carer for Dad I know how difficult both physically and emotionally dementia can be for both the person who has it and close family particularly those who are carers day to day. Relationships can be strained but also strengthened and I truly believe that love conquers all. Despite the pain, the dementia journey can still provide gifts of memories that will last forever.

It is true to say that no one person's dementia journey is exactly the same as anyone else's and it is also true to say that family members who are carers can go through moments of emotional despair when nothing they try to do seems to work.

It occurred to me in writing the book that caring for loved ones, no matter what illness or condition they have, is a similar journey for all carers certainly from an emotional perspective.

The collection of poems in this book is therefore aimed at and inspired by all of those on a caring journey.

It aims to highlight the journey they are on as well as celebrate what they are doing. At the same time it aims to help those on the caring journey through sharing my experiences, and those of others.

I should also add that I will receive no payment for any time or effort in writing the book and that my royalties from the sales of this book will go to Alzheimer's Research UK, the world's largest dedicated dementia research charity, in the hope that it will go some way to helping find a cure which I am sure is the common wish of us all.

Finally, I hope you find this book useful on your journey. If so I would be very grateful if you would leave a review on Amazon, Goodreads, Reedsy or any other forum. It does so much to encourage other readers and to raise funds for dementia research.

Thank You

Pat

Carers

Carers for the young
Carers for the old
Old caring for the young
Young caring for the old
Parents caring for their children
Children caring for their parents
Caring for people with illnesses of the mind
Caring for people with illnesses of the body
Carers unpaid and not recognised
Carers with a vocation and undervalued
Carers unseen with stories often untold
Always remember you are many in number and not on
your own
Share your stories and needs with each other and don't
be alone
Look after your loved one but look after yourself too
What you are doing is wonderful so always stand tall
The poems in this book are to celebrate you one and all

Testimonials

"A wonderful tribute to and celebration of those caring for loved ones and all that they do.

This collection of poems that Pat has written is both touching and uplifting. It shows the key role that Carers have in looking after loved ones with dementia and other conditions.

We're so grateful to Pat for supporting Alzheimer's Research UK. Fantastic fundraising efforts like this collection of poems will help us to make life-changing research breakthroughs for people with dementia."

Bernie Carranza, Regional Fundraising Officer at Alzheimer's Research UK

"McTaggart's poems are a sweet source of comfort, shared experience, and wise advice as he poignantly expresses the joys, the sadness, and the challenges of caregiving, especially for loved ones with dementia. As I also know from my own experiences with my mother and now my aunt, there are moments of great love amidst the despair."

Linda Austin, author of Poems That Come to Mind: For Those Who Love Someone With Dementia.

"The collection offers us an insight like a traveller's guide to the land of dementia, helping us to identify the unknowns and quirks of the scenery and to negotiate the many rocky roads that confront us in every direction, often showing us a way forward that we may not have thought possible.

An invaluable companion for dementia carers young and old, crossing international and emotional boundaries alike, with warmth and charm."

Peter Burgham, Award Winning Poet

"Poems of sincerity and support, written from the heart of experience, which guide, reveal to and warm the reader."

Rachel Deeming, Author, Blogger, Book Reviewer

Alzheimer's Research UK

Alzheimer's Research UK is the UK's leading dementia research charity, dedicated to causes, diagnosis, prevention, treatment and cure. Backed by passionate scientists and supporters, it is challenging the way people think about dementia, uniting the big thinkers in the field and funding the innovative science that will deliver a cure.
It is working across four key areas of action.

- Understand the diseases that cause dementia.

- Diagnose people earlier and more accurately.

- Reduce risk, backed by the latest evidence.

- Treat dementia effectively.

It funds a broad range of research projects to understand dementia and drive us towards better diagnosis, preventions and treatments.
It has invested in over 1000 projects across all forms of dementia since 1998. It has funded thousands of dementia researchers based in more than 100 institutions in the UK and around the world.

Through these important strands of work, it is bringing about breakthroughs that will change lives.
Its vision is a world where people are free from the fear, harm and heartbreak of dementia.

Its mission is to bring about the first life-changing dementia treatment by 2025.

If you would like to know more about Alzheimer's Research UK and the work it does please visit their website:

www.alzheimersresearchuk.org

In aid of

Alzheimer's Research UK

Many Types of Caring

Although a lot of the focus of this book is on caring for a loved one who has dementia, there are many conditions, diseases and illnesses mental and physical which mean a person requires care and this is most often provided by a loved one's family or other relatives. Many of the messages of the poems in this book are common regardless of the condition. This section of the book includes poems on different conditions that I have experience of but there are many, many more and while the nature of the treatment and care for each condition may vary, the emotional journey that the carer is on is very much the same.

My Mum and Dad who inspired many of the poems in
this book.

The Dementia Train

Dad has just boarded the Dementia train
With seats for all the family to share in the pain
More and more carriages are added each day
To make room for the many going this way
The journey may be long and of many stages
But without any stations to make any changes
Most people on board count many years one and all
But some early on-boarders have also heard the call
The windows reflect memories personal and shared
Of the people in the seats with whom they are paired
The music and singing is a joy to behold
With singers and dancers stepping forward so bold
As the journey progresses the windows mist up
Like the connections in the brain that sadly dry up
The memories grow foggy
The journey more rocky
Silence takes over from singing
Loving and caring, caring and loving, loving becomes
caring
Holding hands and hugs till journey's end
Never left to ride alone or in need of a friend

It doesn't come alone ...

It is often said that old age does not come on its own
It brings with it some friends and some foes but never
comes alone
In truth who age will bring as we grow old
Is not something that can easily be foretold
Until time marches on and old age starts to show
It is not something that we will know

The friends we hope old age will bring
Are the things that will make our hearts sing
Good health and good time to enjoy our retirement
The plans we made over many years for our
contentment
For some they may be bold
Running marathons even as they grow old
For others it may be
More time in the caravan by the sea
Spending lots of time with family
Having grandchildren visit and stay over with me
Watching them as they grow up
Joy and happiness in my cup
Enough money not to scrimp and save
To keep warm, eat well and sometimes misbehave

Aches and pains are not unusual foes that old age will bring
We battle through and try not to let them stop us doing lots of things
Some foes though we wish so much that old age had left at home
As a carer for my Mum and Dad I know this from experience of my own

My Mum she finds it difficult to walk, even with sticks and wheels to hold
Legs and feet refuse to do as they are told
Her body is more frail than it used to be
With shoulders hunched as we can all see
Her hand sometimes trembles and her grip is not the same
While arthritis in her back gives so much pain

My Dad was diagnosed with dementia some time ago
A combination of Alzheimers and Vascular as far as we know
His personality has changed in some ways and challenging behaviours sometimes come to the fore
He started to forget things more and more and more
There seems no rhyme nor reason to what or who or how so
But memories have faded somewhat and names of loved ones also

Even then with foes so strong
We must always try and carry on
In beside the pain and the strife

Old age still allows you blessings to pass on love and
wisdom on life

My Mum she never does complain
No matter how much she is in pain
She listens and she chats and she is here for us all
Her smile lights up the room and cheers one and all

In amongst the pain dementia brings, rather than
feeling sad
Take a step back sometimes and try to look very hard
Like a light shining in the darkness you'll find
The Hidden Gifts of Dementia and the Magic of the
Mind
Value tender moments, pearls of wisdom, humour and
the smiles
A collective sense of healing they'll bring and be with
you all the while

One sharp mind one strong body shared between two
Forever a partnership with love always shining
through
For me a carer in my sixtieth year for whom other plans
must wait
I have discovered that to care for those who cared for
us is a great gift and honour to appreciate

Even if the foes old age should bring steal your plans
for the future you hoped would last
Always remember you have memories that reflect the
life you have lived and your past
You must try though to get rid of the dark and create
your own new light

Share your memories with your loved ones that they
may live on and never be out of sight
A memory shared with someone you love it will still
live on
Your legacy to your family and others for long after
you have gone
Make new plans and focus on what you can do still,
that is your future now
Enjoy time with your loved ones and each new day you
can, it is important amidst it all never to forget how

No matter what friends or foes old age should bring to
those we know
We should always look after our elderly, value them
and let our love for them show
With old age comes experience and wisdom they will
happily share
All we need do to receive it is to show how much we
care
Sit down, spend some time, talk with them and listen
too
I guarantee it will bring cups of joy and happiness to
the both of you

Watching Me

One day I saw a little girl standing in my living room -
watching me
She appeared day after day, standing there - watching
me
I spoke to her but she did not answer, just stood there –
watching me
She would not tell me her name so I gave her one –
Molly

As days went by Molly was joined by a woman who
also stood – watching me
They were followed later by other people, men and
women who would not speak
Just stood there – watching me
They appeared from nowhere, in different rooms of the
house, at different times of the day, never saying
anything – just watching me
They have the faces and bodies of people but
sometimes appear on a spike – frightening for me
I never know when they will come or when they will
go
I only know they are unnerving and will be watching
me
No privacy at all when they are always – watching me

These people I see

Are only visible to me
Not to any of my family
Or to anyone who comes to visit me

It seemed amusing at first, just me and Molly
But sometimes now it is frightening for me
And I can't help but worry
What is it that is wrong with me?
I am old and I am frail
Has my mind now also started to fail?

Early one day
The Doctor came to say
The syndrome that I have is named after Charles
Bonnet
It is my eyes that are failing as I grow old
My mind is not to blame I have been told
Incomplete pictures sent to my brain from my eyes
Cause me to hallucinate is what they surmise
Leaving me with some visual exercises to try
The hallucinations I see, are likely to stay
At least for some time is what the Doctor had to say
They have no medicine to give or treatment to make
them go away
At least my mind is still sharp I am happy to say

Blessings

One cold winter some twenty-five plus years ago
My family all caught the cold and sore throat that was
on the go
The sore throat I remember was particularly bad
For Mum it was the worst she'd ever had
For us the cold and sore throat passed
For Mum it just seemed to last
After three sets of antibiotics it was still no better
So it was off to the hospital with a referral letter

On coming home from work one day, my Mum and
Dad were waiting
To give me some news that was quite heart breaking
The Doctors at the hospital had done their testing
Sadly they had found it was Cancer from which Mum
was suffering
My Mum and Dad were calm, no doubt had shed some
tears when they came home
For me the tears started to flow and to compose myself
I needed a short moment on my own
The journey it was starting then
The aim for Doctors and us all to get Mum well again

The treatment prescribed was courses of chemotherapy
Followed later by accompanying radiotherapy
It meant daily visits to hospitals a good few miles away

That seemed to go on for what felt like an eternity
These included the Beatsons in Glasgow which is well known
As a specialist in cancer treatment of some renown
Some of the hospitals were quite run down physically
But the staff were excellent the Doctors especially

The journey it was hard for Mum
The travelling, the stress and the treatment that was to come
Meant sickness, hair falling out, and being physically very ill
Yet the programme of treatment gave little time to sit still
My Mum she remained positive all the way
Fighting hard step by step every single day
My Dad accompanied Mum throughout the journey
Remaining strong, he was Mum's rock, hiding his pain, along the way
That pain was shared by my sister, my brother and myself,
pain which we still remember to this day

I prayed to the Lord, to Our Lady and to Pope John Paul too
I went to Church on Sundays and some week days as well
Please oh please let my Mum get well.

My prayers they were answered, a blessing on our family
The doctors they used their gifts to get Mum back healthy

I prayed again, thank you Lord, Our Lady and Pope
John Paul
For granting this blessing upon us all

As a family we remain thankful that Mum is still with
us today
Walking again together this time on Dad's difficult
journey

Carer so young

Young in years but mind much older
Slight in build but shoulders much broader
Looking after his Mum, who suffers from chronic pain,
and doing all that he can for her
They live on their own, no-one else to look out for her
Getting Mum her breakfast
And her medicines also
Making sure she is comfortable before it is time to go
Taking the bus to school and a full day of classes
Back home late afternoon
Going to the shop on the way home
Oh how time passes
A hug and a smile for Mum and a cup of tea too
He is doing his best to look after you
He misses out on time with friends and the things that
they do
Not that he minds or complains, not something he
would do
Always remember though that Young Carers need care
too

Caring for People with Dementia

The poems in this section are in many ways a continuation of the collection of poems published in my book "Our Dementia Journey" reflecting our family's experience from the perspective of my Dad who has dementia and the family who are on the journey with him. There is a focus on different aspects of caring for those who have dementia and where appropriate some of the poems from the previous collection have been repeated where I felt they offered insight into caring.

Diagnosis

The Consultant's words reverberated like a pinball, echoing through my mind

"I am sorry to have to confirm that you do have dementia"
What does this mean? How will I cope? What do I tell the family?

"I am sorry to have to confirm that you do have dementia"
What will happen to me? When will it happen? What about work?

"I am sorry to have to confirm that you do have dementia"
Why has it happened to me? It can't be right? I am too young?

"I am sorry to have to confirm that you do have dementia"
I want to scream! I want to shout! I want to cry.

"I am sorry to have to confirm that you do have dementia"
Too many questions. Can't take it all in. Too much emotion.
                                  "I want to go home"

The Lost and the Found

Your memory Dear Dad of what has gone before
Is gradually being lost more and more
Your memory of loved ones just the same
Is being lost too including their names
You sometimes forget where home is for you
Yet another thing that is lost sadly it is true
I long for our conversations about work, football and
politics too
Sad as it is, there is nothing we can do
We just try and do the remembering for you

Though Dear Dad you have lost things, you have found
some things anew
They make you happy and give us such pleasure too
Your love of music and singing has come to the fore
The shyness you had isn't there any more
Your memories of songs and the words to them all
You sing and you dance remembering them all
It is so beautiful to see such joy unconfined
The hidden gift of dementia the magic of the mind
They go together the lost and the found

Where do they come from...

Where do they come from?   Where do they go?

The challenging behaviours   that challenge us so.

Are they at sundowning?   Yes but not only so.

The wanting to go home   when already there

The repeating and repeating   and repeating and repeating

The pacing and pacing   walking up and down and round and round

The trailing and trailing   following me wherever I go

The accusing and the blaming   when neither are true

The arguing and the shouting   when neither are like you

And then suddenly they go

Where do they come from?   Where do they go?

I really do not know

The Dementia Storm

The Dementia storm is coming ......
The atmosphere is changing
The Brain Barometer would show pressure rising
The questions are firing
The well meant answers are being met by attitude
Dad's facial expressions are changing
Pacing and pacing
Round and round
The good friends in the mirrors are gone
Replaced by angry men of the storm
Time to batten down the mirrors
Empathise and sympathise
Put Dad's favourite music videos on
Distract and calm as best we can
The question now is how long the storm will last
And when the clear blue sky will reappear
Dad walking into the room singing

What I can remember

I can remember what happened today
But I can't remember what happened yesterday
I can remember what happened some yesteryears
But I can't remember what happened yesterday
Tomorrow I won't remember what happened today
One tomorrow I won't remember what happened
yesterday or today
I may still remember what happened some yesteryears
One tomorrow I won't remember what happened
today or yesterday or in yesteryears
Then I will live in the moment

Free but locked in

Dementia the contradictory disease

Sometimes it seems like it lets you be free
Free from inhibition
Free to soar
Free to dance as if nobody was watching
Free to sing anything
Free to talk to anyone you pass
Free to show new talents that you have
Free from responsibility, things will be done for me
Free from blame – it is the disease not me

But then it locks you in
Locked in to now – gradually forgetting what went
before
Locked in to your mind forgetting names of loved ones
and who they are
Locked in to your body as your senses and physical
abilities gradually go
Locked in physically not able to wander far in case you
can't find your way home

Free to soar but locked in so you can't.

The Wind and the Waves

The winds of dementia beating constantly again, again,
again against the caregiver
Repeating, challenging, following, aggressive winds
Suddenly a wave of emotion rises loudly, angrily, full
of frustration
A cry for help by both the wind and the wave
The call goes out to the family rescuers lifeboat to come
to the aid of us all
Then the wave crashes on to the beach, and slowly runs
up the warm soft sands as the wind stills
The beach strewn with guilt, tiredness, tears and love

Sorry Dad

when I get impatient with you
when I don't understand what YOU are going through
when I try to hurry you along
when I don't listen to YOUR song
when I lose my temper with you
when I am trying so hard not to
when everyday things get in the way
when they stop us making a great day
when I don't see what is bothering you or giving you
pain
when I can't make it go away and not come back again
when I feel so tired and frail
when despite doing my best for you I fail

but ...
I will always remember the real you.
I hope you can find it in your heart to forgive me as
much as I love you

Smile

Living alongside dementia can be difficult and trying
Challenging behaviours may sometimes make you
angry
And other times make you feel like crying
Each day will have its ups and its downs
Its highs and its lows
Its smiles and its frowns
Sometimes it is Dad's beaming loving smile in the
midst of it all
That makes it all worthwhile and for you to keep
answering the call

Autumn

I sit here at the window, now in my autumn years
Looking out at the garden tree behind the glass veneer
The summer view of green now fading to autumn's
brown and gold

I watch the leaves falling slowly, wistfully to the
ground
I feel sad as they remind me of the memories I have
lost, never to be found
The tree, like me, is now but a shadow of its summer
self

A tear drops from my eye, and my wife leans over and
wipes it away
Darling don't be sad she says, holding on to my hand
We still have each other and together we'll enjoy each
new autumn day

The Dementia Winds

The Dementia winds blow
Through Dad's mind, our family, our home
Gently
At first
Softly blowing a few memories away
Then more and more and more as time goes on
Invisible
But always there
The winds can be winds of change
Some bring periods of seeming calm, or sleep
Then the winds come from a different direction
Catching us unawares
The winds blow stronger letting us know they are still
there
Creating emotion, strange behaviours, frustration,
anger, argument
Then they drop down again leaving sadness, tears,
guilt
The only way to keep the dementia winds at bay
Is to wrap a family blanket of love round Dad
The winds then drop down
… But never go away

Great Day

Today is a great day
But I haven't been far away
Neither have I been on holiday
And I haven't won the lottery
It is not Christmas Day or Easter Day
Neither is it my birthday
Infact I have been at home all day
Spending time with Dad and the family
Dad is happy, chatting, joking, smiling, singing and
dancing
That's what makes it a great day

Non-awareness

My Dad has dementia but of this he is unaware
They call it "non awareness" and I am told it is not that
rare
Yet despite this there are certainly moments in time
When I think Dad has an incline
That things are not quite fine
Like when he asks Mum if he has done something
wrong, just a feeling
Or when he seems to know he has forgotten how to do
something
It is as if the fog lifts from time to time
Albeit just for a moment at a time

Sleep

Too little sleep
Too much sleep
Sleeping during the day
Not sleeping at night
Not sleeping during the day
Sleeping at night
Sleeping some of the day
Sleeping some of the night
In a light sleep
In a deep sleep
A broken sleep
Which should it be?
It doesn't' just affect me
It affects the whole family
It affects my moods
It affects my behaviour
Which combination will be our saviour?

Same but Different

You are my Dad .... I am your Son
We both look the same as we have always done
You love me .... I love you
Just the same as we have always done
We chat .... and we laugh
Just the same as we have always done

Your mind is different .... and mine is too
Logic is gone .... and emotions to the fore
That is different to how it used to be
You forget things now .... I remember for you
That is different to how it used to be
You follow me now .... I used to follow you
That is different to how it used to be
You get upset easily and sometimes shout ....it isn't
always clear to me what it is all about
That is different to how it used to be
When the sun is going down you find it
difficult........as do I now
That is different to how it used to be

We are different .... but still the same
Behind the challenging behaviours and my reactions to
them
Behind the forgetfulness too
You are still you nonetheless and I am still me
We are the same .... but different

The Dementia Spell

Dementia casts its spell affecting the mind and the
senses as well
It affects what we smell
And what we taste too
It affects what we see
And what we hear as well
It affects what we feel, hot and cold
Not a sense untouched as we grow old

No Sense

Even though my eyes are healthy with no abnormality
I still cannot always recognise faces, places and objects
visually
I look and see great danger that I must step over
But it is only the carpet next to the tiles in one room to
another
Some days as well I see things I am told are not really
there
And I need colour coded signs and bold contrasts to
help go anywhere

Even though my nose is healthy and I thought it
worked just fine
Apparently I can't smell smoke if something is burning
in the toaster or on the ring
Food smells good to me but sometimes it is off
Bottles I thought were drinks and smell good to me
turn out to be for cleaning

Even though my mouth, tongue and taste buds all seem
good
What I eat now in terms of food
Is different to what I traditionally ate
Things I used to like I now hate
Nobody knows what to put on my plate

Even though the Audiologist said my hearing was
good

It is true to say that there are sometimes words and
sounds that I have not always understood
Noise in the background or words coming at me too
fast
Have caused me difficulty now and in the past

Even though what I touch and feel seems to me ok
I don't like cold water running on my hand and away
I tend to touch hot plates and pots be sure they are hot
enough
I like things to be smooth and not rough
I also like people to hold my hand but get a fright if
people touch me by surprise

All of this makes no sense to me at all
It is all in the mind apparently
Just another thing Dementia brought me when she
came to call

Living Alongside Dementia

Living alongside Dementia can be challenging for all
It is always important therefore to remember things
you must do and others not at all
Don't get impatient when Dad repeats again and again
and again
Don't get frustrated when you have to show Dad the
way over and over again
Don't get upset, when Dad doesn't remember who you
are
Don't complain when Dad doesn't know how to buckle
up when in the car
Don't argue with Dad, logic will never convince him
Don't tell Dad he is wrong you will only upset him
Don't get annoyed when Dad doesn't understand
Don't shout or lose your temper even if you are finding
things difficult to withstand
Do show love and kindness in everything you do
Do imagine yourself in Dad's shoes and think how he
would help you
Do reassure Dad when he seems upset though it may
not be clear why
Do remain calm at all times even if you have to count to
ten and really, really try
Do let your body language be aligned to the calmness
Do make sure you do this otherwise just kind words
are pointless

Do try and see what is upsetting Dad it may be pain
unmentioned
Do look hard to find the reason, that there always is
one should be unquestioned
Do respond to the emotion expressed rather than the
behaviour on the go
Do be kind to yourself as well Dad would want it to be
so
There are may do's and many don'ts to help us all keep
going
Just do your best, and always remember, that's what
Dad is doing.

Vera Says

There are different techniques suggested and VERA[1] is
just one
That help to interact with those who have dementia
including a loved one
Validate what they are saying is the start
Address the **Emotion** they are feeling is the next
important part
Reassuring them has a very important part to play
Then focus thereafter on **Activity**

Paula[2] who knows the Wizards of Alz, has a simple
technique which is:
In very basic terms to think "Why this? Try this"
It may sound too simple
But I have found it very useful
It forces you to think what is driving behaviour
Then to try different ways to shift that behaviour
Reassure, Review the cause, Remove any triggers,
Redirect is just a part
But it can certainly help if used together with a loving
heart

For some things in life putting your head down and
fighting through
Can often be very much the right thing for you to do

But in dealing with dementia I suggest it is better "to go round and not go through"
Logic is out the window, and no argument you will win
You may cause further upset and just heighten emotion
Take a step to the side and view it from there
Try a different tact or go a different way, there will be one for sure
You'll get there much quicker if you remain fleet of mind and thought
Even when sadly your loved one is not

References:
1.VERA is a communication framework background developed by Blackhall et al. (2011)
2. Paula refers to Paula Spencer Scott who wrote an excellent book "Surviving Alzheimers" which references the "Wizards of Alz" in the first chapter.

Find your sycamore tree

Caring for a loved one with dementia can be
challenging we know
Many things will happen that you don't understand
and wonder how so?
Behaviours may be perplexing and challenging too
You may feel that whatever you say or do is not getting
through
But however tempting it may be dear friend please
don't give up

The answer may be to seek a different perspective
Step to the side and try going round and not going
through
It may help you both get to where you want to
There will inevitably be some logic somewhere there
you see
Or actions caused by pain you did not know your loved
one has
Seek a different vantage point or your own sycamore
tree to look down from
Ask the right questions, be patient and think hard as
well
Give your loved one a chance to tell

The centre of your universe

When you start caring for a loved one there is a lesson
you must quickly learn
If you do not then the frustration that builds will be
long term
At first I thought I could schedule things in nice little
time slots
But unfortunately no matter how I tried I found I could
not
It just leads to frustration and trying to hurry your
loved one along
It is the opposite of what is needed and is completely
wrong
You may try to fit things round your work and your
play
But very soon you will learn it does not work that way
In days of old people thought the sun revolved round
the earth
They were of course wrong and you will also find you
are no longer the centre of your universe
Accept the way things are and make changes in your
life
Lean in to love and give your loved one their best life
The only control you will have is over the changes you
choose to make
Putting your loved one at the centre is the best decision
you can take

Working from that starting point will make things
easier it is true
Then build your life around this including making time
for you
Focus then on making the journey for your loved one
the best you can do

Love Dad in his "now"

Love and appreciate Dad as he is now
What Dad believes, understands, knows, remembers
now
Will be different to last year
Or even yesterday, despite it being so near
And will be different tomorrow and next year
Love and appreciate Dad in his "now"
Though it may be a "moveable feast"
You will find it makes things easier somehow
Dad's world on any day may be different to yours
Don't try and correct him or worse still argue
Focus on making him happy and feel good about
himself
That is when you will be happy and feel good yourself

Driving with Dementia

Dad liked driving in his car
Sometimes journeys short sometimes journeys far
When dementia first came
Dad declared to DVLA the condition, driving remained
the same
As time went on some small things started to go wrong
Getting the right gear, going a little near
Then we started to fear
How do you stop someone driving who has been
driving for years
Taking away mobility
Taking away independence
Replacing with a bus pass and reliance
Emotional for all
Dual dilemma of how and when to make that call
For us age marched on before it became too bad
Time to renew the driving licence says the government
Medical checks needed and Dad called a halt to it all
Much to the relief of us all we never had to make that
call

Turning Back the Clock

It will soon be Halloween
So we need to reset our Time Machine
Yours as well as ours
Put them back by just one hour
There is something to be said
For that extra hour in bed

But if you have dementia
This small change I confess
Can sometimes cause confusion
And lead to much distress

Things you could try to avoid the Halloween fright
In the morning go outside or be exposed to sunlight
Have a daytime routine and one as well at night
Use a clock that shows clearly what is Day and what is
Night
Though these changes may be slight
They may just help keep the body clock right

Dementia a world condition

After another difficult dinnertime today
No doubt impacted by sundowning in some way
I then switched on the TV to watch the news of the day

Watching the terrible scenes from the Ukraine
They gave me real cause to wonder
What people living there with dementia are enduring
in pain
Along with their caregivers and who will save them
from going under

That lead me to ponder
About dementia the world over
Living with and alongside dementia can be challenging
for all
But how much more difficult in countries where there
are no support services at all
How do they feel and how do they cope?
Do they understand and do they have any hope?

Dementia is a global condition
Forecast to get worse beyond current recognition
Peoples of the world must unite
Put dementia in the spotlight and fight
For funds to provide the research needed
Making sure the warnings are heeded

We need hope the world over that a cure will be found
And the drugs will be shared all around
In countries from A to Z
No matter where they may be

The Scientists

The scientists work by day and by night
Doing their tests to get things right
Trying so hard to find the light

Looking for ways to early diagnose
Looking for ways to prevent and slow the disease
Looking for ways to calm us and make us feel at ease

Looking too to find a cure
Then the future will be bright for sure

Carers' Lives

The poems below try to give an insight into the lives of those caring for loved ones. Each person's journey is different but has a lot in common especially from an emotional perspective. Nothing can totally prepare you for the journey but love and faith and hope are what help you to carry on.

A Carer's Life

Life as a Carer can take its toll
Working so hard each day and sometimes night as well
Stress and worry about your loved one and no-one to
tell
Lacking in sleep and getting more tired each day
No time to look after yourself or chase the blues away
If you feel it has to be this way
It may be time to talk to Carers UK
You will find this can help in many a way ...

A Carer's Routine

A Carer's routine is often the same every day
No weekends or bank holidays changing things in any
way
They are there ready for their loved one wakening up
Their day does not end till their loved one goes to sleep
Sometimes as well a nightshift they must work or be on
call
Should their loved one need anything at all
They don't do it for any payment or allowance
They do it out of love and faith and hope provide
endurance

Carer care for thy self

You care for your loved one by day and by night
You are doing your best, I know I am right
You are tired and sometimes lonely but tell no-one at
all
Always ready to answer your loved one's call

You have little or no time for yourself
To catch up with friends, take a holiday or just enjoy
life
You often worry and also stress
You are doing all you can but what about your rest?

You must Dear Carer take time to look after yourself
Be assured that is what your loved one would want as
well
If you do not then you put at risk your health
Then for your loved one you will be no good at all
Who will then look after you all?

Hold out your hand and ask for help
To family or friends or social services or charities
They will you will find be pleased to help
The relief you will feel as with them you share
Shows even more just how much you do care

A Carer's Plea

Do you feel some days that you can't cope?
Are you tempted then to give up hope?
Are you ever lacking in sleep?
Do you feel you are in too deep?
Are you moody, grumpy and guilty?
Does it seem like you have forgotten how to smile?
Or at least you haven't done so for a while?
Always remember then that tomorrow's a new day
God will help you if you pray
Someone will lend you a hand if you just say
So you can take a rest
Caring is not meant to be a test
Keep the faith and never give up hope
Remember why you do it, you do it out of love
Smile at what you have achieved and the kindness you
show
Look after your loved one but yourself also

Carer So Caring

Carer so kind
Carer so patient
Carer so tolerant
Carer so tender
Carer so gentle
Carer so loving
Carer so faithful
Carer so loyal
Carer so hard working
Carer so self sacrificing

Carer so tired
Carer so emotional
Carer so worried
Carer so stressed
Carer so alone
Carer so sad
Carer so needing help

Carer so caring
Carer still caring

New Day Dawning

Caring for a loved one
can mean good days
and bad days
By all means learn from a bad day
But do not dwell on it
Or feel guilty in any way
Look instead at each new dawning
As a chance to make it
A Great Day

Lucky Me

As a carer for both Mum and Dad
Some well meaning people tell me your Mum and Dad
are lucky to have you there
That is where I must disagree
I am what Mum and Dad made me to be
The love they have shown, the example they set,
always being there for me
That is what fashioned me
It is a privilege and honour to look after Mum and Dad
To learn from them still as the wisdom and memories
they pass on
The smiles and the laughter amidst it all
It is me that is the luckiest of all

Tough Times

At some points on the Carer's journey they will feel they cannot cope or are at the end of their tether.

The poems below reflect these times and the emotions I know I felt and also ways to carry on.

Guilt

Guilt when you can be there
Guilt when you cannot
Guilt when you can do something
Guilt when you cannot
Guilt when you said something that you wish you
hadn't
Guilt when you didn't say something that you wish
you had
Guilt when you did something that you wish you
hadn't
Guilt when you didn't do something that you wish you
had
Guilt during the daytime
Guilt during the night-time
Guilt as a call to action led by your conscience
Guilt as regret and hope when you did not follow your
conscience
Guilt sapping energy from you as a wasted emotion
Guilt in whatever form it comes means it's time to take
positive action
Time to follow your conscience and do what you
should, or
Time to try and make amends in whatever way you
think you still could,
Resolving that next time you will do all that you should

Silent Scream

A silent scream
You know what I mean
Sometimes it is needed, to let off steam
It is loud and it is clear
But no one can hear
And it is nothing to fear
It can help with your sanity
And sometimes bring clarity
Releasing emotions from within
Letting calmness back in
Best done in your private place
Where no-one can see your face
You are after all only part of the human race

Crying room

Caring for loved ones of ages young and old
Is an emotional roller coaster with stories often untold
Moments of great joy, accompany moments of great
pain
For those living this life it can be so hard to explain
Loving and caring, caring and loving, loving becoming
caring
Love and joy, laughter and happiness
Pain and sadness, hopes and regret
Anger and impatience, tiredness and guilt

Churches have their children's crying rooms
Madrid has La Lloreria
The Pope has his "Room of Tears"
Carers too need their private place, somewhere they
can go
To allow the tears to flow sometimes and to let the
emotions go
When they come out of their "crying room" they are
hopefully calmer than before
Ready once more to carry on and put their loved one to
the fore

Faith, Hope and Love

When you accompany a loved one on their dementia
journey
It strikes me that you need faith in many ways

You need faith in the doctors and nurses who are well
trained in what they do
That doesn't mean you should never question them as
nobody knows your loved one better than you.
Medication is needed when it will do good but no harm
But sometimes a "fiblet" can be better than a tablet to
keep your loved one calm

You need faith in your loved one that they are doing
their best
They are not trying to make the journey a trial or a test
Nobody can imagine just what they are going through
And it is never their intention to make things difficult
for you

You need faith in your family and friends supporting
you
You will often need to lean on them when you don't
know quite what to do
They may sometime say things that you may not want
to hear

But it is only because they have your interests at heart
and love you dear

You need faith in yourself that you too are doing your
best
And sometimes you need and are entitled to take a rest
Don't be too hard on yourself when it is a difficult time
You may get things wrong sometimes but will get them
right next time
Trying to make each day the best it can be for your
loved one is what you try to do
And nobody can ask any more of you

You need faith in God above that he will look after you
and your loved one too
Only God knows what's round the corner and what's
in front of you
Never try to work it out or ask why me or why us it is a
logic of which we are not capable
Simply trust that you will not have to cope with any
more than you are able
Looking back on your journey you may find only one
footprint in the sand
Where God was carrying you both I am sure you
understand

Never give up hope and each day is a new day
And always remember love will see you through most
things you have to do
The love you show your loved one, love for God and
love for you

Friends

The journey we are on with Dad is very much a family affair with both Mum and Dad at the centre and with myself, my sister Donna and her family, and my brother Steven and his family.

In addition the support of friends can also be a great help both to carers and their loved ones. The smallest of things can make a big difference...

Poem from a Friend

I received a poem by email from a friend (to be)
It came in the middle of the night (and it troubled me)
Great pain was on the page for all to see
Tears falling as she sent the poem to me
She looked after her Mum throughout her Dementia
Journey
A journey so hard it took its toll on her Mum, her
brother and she
Even although her Mum was now safe and free
My friend was still in pain and so sad about:
"Dementia and all it has taken from me"
She was reaching out to someone on a similar journey

Still today the sadness has not gone
Her loving memories of her Mum they will always live
on
She keeps herself busy as she tries to move on
She is back in the choir, singing many a song
She looked for a new job, it didn't take her long
She is caring and sharing to friends new and life long
Her Mum would be so proud as she looks on
She deserves to be happy I am sure it won't be long

Flower Lady

The Flower Lady comes and leaves flowers for Mum
and Dad on the step
She doesn't come in because they are shielding from
Covid you see
Rain hail or shine she brings flowers regularly
Each time that she comes it brightens their day
Roses and carnations, chrysanthemums sometimes,
And a flowering red poinsettia at Christmastime
All delivered with love whatever the time of year

The Flower Lady has had her own trials and sadness
and grief
Caring and loving and nursing whenever it was needed
Losing children when they were still too young
Losing parents and husband too
Sadness so great it would break many people
But she carries on with faith sharing her love for others

Dear Flower Lady you know who you are
God bless you forever wherever you are

Reflections by Carers

It is often said that everyone has a book in them. Whether or not that is true I do believe it is certainly true that everyone has a poem in them.

It doesn't matter whether you have never written a poem before, I hadn't until recently. It also doesn't matter what your writing skills are as poems are often about the spoken word and can be written as they are spoken.

In my last book I encouraged everyone to take some time out and sit down and write or speak a poem. You may well find it therapeutic and it may also give you a sense of satisfaction when it is done. It may well let you express your feelings in a way you can't necessarily do any other way.

I believe that poetry has a great deal to offer those living with dementia and their families and caregivers. Both in terms of expressing their creativity and indeed in reading and sharing it.

I was delighted that many people did indeed send me their poems and so this section includes just some of those poems from those who have experience of caring for loved ones with dementia and their reflections and insights. I thank them for their willingness to share these very personal and often poignant thoughts to try and help others.

My Mum

By Clare Melia

You were always there for me!
Come rain or shine.
You said it " would be fine"!
As you held my hand.
Held me close.
Helped me to understand.
When I cried the most.
You were always there.
You did nothing but care.
For me-and our family.

Then you went away
Into a foreign land
That no one could understand
Least of all you!
You were sad and blue.
Forgot how to be.
Forgot even me!
And what we'd been through.

You were as stranger
Losing her way.
Fading every day
Every thing was new.

Every person you met -
Someone you'd forget.
Every thing an issue.
Every moment causing pain.
Driving me insane!

You're up and you're down!
Roaming everywhere!
Looking for things
Falling from your chair.
Won't go to bed!
Can't get up!
Forgotten how to eat.
Can't hold a cup.

I get no sleep!
For nearly two years!
I have to go to work.
Often in tears.
My brother cares for you
While I'm away
When I come home
He goes to bed.
I have you instead
For the rest of the day.

You won't eat
You won't sleep
You won't sit still
You won't take your pill!
You're up and you're down
You drive me insane!
Where do I go with all of this pain?!

Then one day you are no more
You lie in your bed
I think that you are dead
We call an ambulance
They take you away
To the hospital
We visit every day

They want you to come home
Back to our flat
We look at each other
We can't have that!
We can't cope any more
We're battered and we're sore
So you have to go away
We cannot have you stay

We're sad and we're blue
We visit all we can
You sit in your bed
We stroke your head
We touch your hand
We love you so much
Can you feel our touch?

You lie and you cry!
You make me want to die!
I feel so guilty it hurts
To see you like this
You won't eat
You can't talk
You can smile

You can't walk

They look after you
Instead of us two.
They seem to care
They are always there
They say you are fine
Even though you are mine.

I cry - even now!
When you are safe and free
We did our best
To look after you
-though it wasn't meant to be.

You're with Dad now and the rest
Of the family.
I hope you are happy
Now that you are free?
I hope you understand
That we did all that we could.
How I hate 'Dementia"!
And all it has taken from me......

Living Grief

By Clare Melia

I go to work
and laugh and play.
I chat with my friends
throughout the day.
But when I come home
I'm all on my own.
My brother's in bed.
My thoughts rule my head.

I have a glass - or two! - of wine.
It helps to pass the time.
I can't be bothered to eat.
I'm too upset-and
drink is a safer bet.

You are not here!
But you are everywhere!
Your teddies and dolls.
Your books and photos.
Your room left untouched.
Your bed still made.
I lie on it and cry!
All I can do is sigh.

Phone the Care Home

to see how you are.
You're doing 'ok' -
could be better.
Not eating or drinking much.
Nothing to worry about.
They'll be in touch.

I see you every week.
It's heart-breaking to be sure.
We have to do a 'test'.
Wait for the results.
Try and be cheerful.
Talk to your Carers,
who sometimes can't tell us the truth.
Although I can see it in their eyes -
they do not lie.

You are lying in your bed.
Music on the radio.
I kiss the side of your head.
You wake up and look at me
with such love!
As if I'm an Angel from up above!

Your eyes are shining brightly,
as you stare at me.
Your smile is 'joyous'
as if you cannot believe who you see!
How often have you lain here
thinking of me?

I live with my grief,
although you are not dead.

I hate the thoughts that go around my head.
How long will it take
to stop all this pain?
For you-and-for me.
I will never be the same again.□

My Dementia Journey

By Clare Melia

My "Dementia Journey" is not the same as yours.
It is full of heartache and despair.
It howls in the night without a care.
It cuts into my heart and tears me apart.
It makes me cry out loud
and wraps a cloud -
around my heart.
Never to depart.

'Grief' is a thief
that comes night and day.
Like an 'old friend'
It is never far away.
It takes me by surprise
Every time.
It breaks this fragile heart of mine.

Tears rush to my eyes!
I don't know why?
They come without warning
and take my breath away.

My heart beats faster!
I think I'm going to die.
I rush off in a panic.

I have to run away.

'Grief' follows me around.
It has a hold upon my heart.
It won't let me go -
no matter that I know
It will always be there
to remind me
how much I care.

Nanny

By Rachel Deeming

It has been a long time since you have left.
My life is very different now.
You would not know me, I doubt
As the little girl who liked jam sandwiches.
I wish you could see me and my boys.
I think they'd love you.

I like to remember you as I remember being small.;
A little girl in white socks with scuffed knees
The socks the same height as your Corgi;
Holding your hand as we walked together.
Skirts with thick material and sensible colours.
A solid presence – my nanny.
White-haired and caring, I hear your voice in my head.
It's not often that I try to hear it.
I should try more, try harder;
But it went a long time ago, even while you were still
here.

You were taken before you died;
Your mind lost to somewhere else,
Somewhere you could not be reached.
You were still Nanny but not Nanny too;
A pretender, a person unknown to me.
I wish you were here now.

I wish that I could know you.
I wish that I could remember more before.
Before you became remote.

I go back to that walk in the woods.
It reminds me of you. You are there in the scents
And the rough ground.
It was a place that you showed me;
Green, magical, hidden bridge in the reeds;
the remnants of an earl's life
With a boathouse in the trees.
I love that you took me there.
I love that I know that, can hold it in my head.
I love that I can go there and think about you
As my nanny and not a hospital visit.
That place is beautiful but more, it's you.

Widow of a Living Man

By Sonja Lamb

The only words I hear,
And they're music to my ear,
Are the ones each night
When I say, "Sleep tight".

And I fervently hope
I'll be able to cope
For as long as I can
For the love of one man.

At times it's too much
To never feel a loving touch,
To never be hugged tight
In the middle of the night.

So the days drag on,
And the nights are long,
But I'll ride this wave,
I'll be strong … I'll be brave.

Today

By Alison Miller

Today
Will it be today
that you forget me?

Tomorrow
Will it be today
that you forget me?

Future
Will it be today
that you forget
who you are?

Will it be...

Stormy Night, Stormy Mind

By Alison Miller

"I dreamed last night
That my body left here…"
He waved his arms
outstretched.

"Left the home?" my laugh
ricochets around his room.

"It was so real, but my mind was so confused…"

"Maybe a stormy dream…"
I mused,
"or a temperature
from Covid?"

"It was so real…"

"But your body's still here!"
my heart whimpers,
"and your mind's elsewhere…"

Time to be Present

By Caroline Devenish-Meares

As the dawn is breaking
The rising of the sun has just begun
The troubles of yesterday are behind
The day is new
It is time to be present
Feel the wind in your hair
Feel the sun on your back
Taste the flavours of nature's produces
Enjoy the smells of nature's fragrances
The heart will be heavy from loss
The pain will be calling It is your time to be present
The power of now is with you
Be present in the moment Look for the positives in your
loss
There are gifts our loved ones have left behind
The love they shared
The good times of great experiences they dared
The lessons they gave us
The warmth of their love and friendship
Guidance for the person you are today
 They live on in us with their words
The dawn is breaking
 The rising of the sun has just begun
It is your time to be present
Time to be present in the moment.

I'm A Happy Alzheimers Poem

By Sangita Kansal

Dad kept on, he knew the Indian Prime Minister
Ebulliently adding they studied together
Daily repetition signalled early dementia
Other stories regurgitated thereafter

After meals he would forget
'I haven't eaten yet'
Grumbling I was a selfish daughter
Saying 'You give my apple pies away' causing
laughter

His mind began to go, I was his carer
A dramatic change with Alzheimers
Viscerally I was distraught
A bleak future plagued my thoughts

Fortuitously the deterioration wasn't fast
Merrily he boarded buses with a pass
We received good support
His childish joy infused me with comfort

But he refused to bathe or shower
I paid a professional carer
Showed dad written notes, If he didn't clean
He would be fined for lack of hygiene

Unable to grasp he smelt
'Do I stink?' he asked some friends
They were too embarrassed and polite
To my father's distorted delight

Angrily blamed our aunt Jasvinder
For stealing his broken umbrella
Just hours after, with affection rang her
As if nothing had happened

Always wore pyjamas under his trousers
Relished a monkey like fetish for bananas
Would not easily accept new clothes
Attached to the old kept saying 'No'

Over time required a commode
Or his night clothes soaked
Lived in his own fantasy world
Reality increasingly blurred

There was a hidden gem for me
A dementia sufferer can be happy
Dad played cards, chatted, drank copious tea
Attending socials all through his eighties

I Can Still Remember

By Christina Kinney

Inspired by Mrs Helen Kinney

I may not be the same, but you remain the same to me,
I may not look myself, but the changes I don't see,
I may not hear your voices, and remember who you are,
I may not speak as I once did, but my voice remains intact.

I may not like the things now I once adored and loved,
I may not share your memories, but I still feel our love,
I may not much resemble the woman I used to be,
I may not wish, however, to be treated differently.

I may not express emotions, or be what you expect of me,
I may not be entertaining, or participate equally,
I may not be irreplaceable, and seem disposable at best,
I may not be included fairly, as my illness represents my identity, lest.

I may not be the first option, and inconvenient for most I test,
I may not contribute as expected, so I'm pushed out the way instead,

I may not be able to always attend, or have to leave before the end,
I may not be suitable for everything, and this I do know and accept.

I can, however, notice who is really there, as I am still a person in each and every way,
I can still use my eyes, seeing it all unfold galore,
I can still use my ears, but now, hear clearly and take in more,
I can still use my voice, but speak with only trusted friends.

I may be someone different. but some things remain the same,
I may be different looking, but please don't remind me,
I no longer visualise the girl you know to see,
I may be hard of hearing and mix up who you are, but I know I hold you dearly and remember how special you are,
I may not sound the same. and say things I never would, but this is who I am now, just give me help and love.

I may like different things now, and hate things I once loved, just go with it, I promise my smile will show it's worth,
I may not have my memories, but share with me again, and know I love you dearly even though it's tough,
I may resemble the opposite of who I used to be, but know that I am happy living the end of my life the way I want it to be.

I may have blank emotions, and seem to feel so numb,
but I still feel and know what's real,
I may be dull and boring, but I still enjoy fun, even just
in presence, my work is never done,
I may be easily replaceable, but enjoy me while you
can, and I'm still here,
I may be seen as just an illness, but I'm still a person,
treat me fair.

I may be the last option, but I'm first to those that
matter most,
I may be such a hindrance, but including me will make
my day engrossed,
I may be unreliable and not always show face, but
always still invite me, plans easily change,
I may be unsuitable to always have a place, I already
accept this, but know I must say,
I am still my own person, so remember when you can,
treat me as before, no different if you can.

You can however be, the person who is there, and
treats me as an equal with freedom left to spare,
You can still use your eyes, to clearly read me, and look
between the lines to see what I see,
You can still use your ears, to wisely hear the secrecy,
You can still use your voice, but now, to advocate for
me.

I am not just an illness.
I am not just what you see.
1 am still a full person.
I am still the same me.

Everyone Has a Poem

As noted in the previous section I believe that poetry has a great deal to offer those living with dementia and their families and caregivers and indeed caregivers in general where they are looking after loved ones with other conditions.

As you will know, author royalties from this book go to Alzheimer's Research UK and I have received no payment for writing the book.

I would like anyone who wishes, to send me a poem, or poems, particularly those in the Dementia community. It doesn't need to be about dementia and can be about anything as there is still life outside dementia and the creativity of people with dementia and their families, caregivers and those involved with dementia research, support and charities is great.

Depending on the volume of poems I will publish a quarterly collection of some of the poems and send them out to all subscribers for a small subscription and publish a poetry book annually with a lot more of the poems. Again all royalties will go to dementia charities and all poems published will have full accreditation to their authors in the quarterly collection and annual book.

The hope is that as more and more people find confidence and enjoyment in writing poems and write them more regularly and the publications can become an ongoing thing and raise regular much needed funds for dementia charities.

Please e-mail all poems to:

Pat@Poemsfordementia.com

Website: www.poemsfordementia.com

All poems must be your own work as we want to respect others' privacy and not infringe copyright. By submitting a poem you are agreeing you are the author and you are giving permission for us to publish it as described above.

Go on, give it a go, you know you have it in you! ☐

Finally, I really hope that you have found the book helpful and enjoyed reading some of the poems. It would be great if you could leave a review on Amazon, Goodreads, Reedsy or any other forum which would help encourage others to read it and raise additional funds for Alzheimer's Research.

Thank you

Pat

About the Author

Pat McTaggart is a qualified accountant and spent 25+ years as a Finance Director/CFO and most recently joint CEO within the IT and Software sectors.
He has a strong interest in social enterprise and the charitable sectors and sat on the Board of two charities. Over the last three years Pat has been full time carer for his mum and for his dad, who has dementia, living with them in their home in Scotland.

In 2022 he published a collection of poems in the book "Our Dementia Journey" charting his family's experiences with dementia since his dad's diagnosis.

He is a member of AlzAuthors who are renowned worldwide for their collection of literature and the work they do sharing Alzheimer's and dementia stories to light the way for others and striving to eliminate the stigma surrounding the most important disease of our generation.

He also founded Poems for Dementia aimed at using poetry to help raise funds for Dementia Research.

He can be contacted at:

pat@poemsfordementia.com
Twitter: @pat_mct
www.poemsfordementia.com

Available on Amazon:

https://mybook.to/Bma48Rt

The Purple Angel

The Purple Angel shown below and appearing on the cover of this book in stamp form symbolises a guardian over those living with dementia, their families and friends and those helping to raise awareness of the disease. The Purple Angel Logo became embraced by individuals and organisations across the world and so the globe was added to show the impact and collaboration of this movement.

Now there is one symbol representing a global message RAISING AWARENESS, HOPE AND EMPOWERMENT
For all people living with dementia, their families and care partners.

Links to more information:

Purple Angel Project (alzheimersspeaks.com)
About Us – Purple Angels Global (purpleangel-global.com)

Printed in Great Britain
by Amazon

39156722R00056